A day in the life of a
Storm Chaser

Pierce Feirtear

OXFORD
UNIVERSITY PRESS

OXFORD
UNIVERSITY PRESS

Great Clarendon Street, Oxford OX2 6DP

Oxford University Press is a department of the University of Oxford.
It furthers the University's objective of excellence in research, scholarship,
and education by publishing worldwide in

Oxford New York

Athens Auckland Bangkok Bogotá Buenos Aires Calcutta
Cape Town Chennai Dar es Salaam Delhi Florence Hong Kong Istanbul
Karachi Kuala Lumpur Madrid Melbourne Mexico City Mumbai
Nairobi Paris São Paulo Singapore Taipei Tokyo Toronto Warsaw

with associated companies in Berlin Ibadan

Oxford is a registered trade mark of Oxford University Press
in the UK and in certain other countries

Published in the United Kingdom
by Oxford University Press

Text © Pierce Feirtear 2000

British Library Cataloguing in Publication Data

Data available

ISBN 0 19 915710 3

Available in packs
Weather Pack of Six   (one of each book)   ISBN 0 19 915711 1
Weather Class Pack   (six of each book)   ISBN 0 19 915712 X

Printed in Hong Kong

Acknowledgements

The Publisher would like to thank the following for permission
to reproduce photographs:

Corbis: front cover; Frank Lane Picture Agency/D. Hoadley: title page,
p 20; National Severe Storms Laboratory: p 4 (top); National Geographic
Society/Joseph Bailey: p 4 (bottom).

Illustrations by Julian Baker and David Kearney.

Contents

The storm chaser

My name is Robert Davies-Jones.
I work for the National Severe
Storms Laboratory (NSSL) in
the United States of America.
I am a **scientist**. My job is to
find out about storms so we can
warn people about them. I am
very interested in storms that
cause tornadoes.

On Thursday 8th June 1995, I set
out to chase a storm. This is what
happened.

Tornadoes are huge
windstorms. They can
tear up trees, knock
down houses, and kill
people and animals.
The United States of
America is hit by more
tornadoes than any
other country in the
world.

The forecast

I had a meeting with some other scientists. We knew there were going to be big storms 350 km away. There could be tornadoes too. We were going to chase them.

The car

We hurried to the cars. The weather was fine, but it was still early in the day.

FACT BOX

Most tornadoes happen in spring and early summer. Warm sea air hits cold air from the north, and thunderstorms break out. Sometimes tornadoes drop down out of thunderstorms.

The turtles

We put four turtles into the back of the car. Turtles have instruments inside them which measure the size and strength of tornadoes. We hoped to place them in front of the tornado so it would go over them. Then the turtles could measure the tornado.

No one knows exactly how tornadoes are formed. If we knew, we could give people better warnings about them.

All the cars set out together. There were 20 of them. We had radios to keep in contact with the NSSL and the other cars.

There was a **satellite** in the sky. It would photograph the storms as they grew. There were also two planes in the sky. They would record how much rain and wind were in the storms.

The weather station

A small weather station had been fixed on to the roof of my car. It had an anemometer and a thermometer. The anemometer was to measure the speed of the wind. The thermometer was to measure the **temperature** of the air.

I could read this information on my lap-top computer as we drove along. I sent the information to the team leader in another car. He sent it back to the NSSL.

Storm clouds

I saw the huge storm clouds ahead. They were swirling round and round in the wind. I was not sure if there would be a tornado. If there was, we would see the swirling clouds drop very close to the ground.

In a storm, warm air meets cold air. The warm air rises and begins to spin round and round. The clouds swirl around with it. A big storm like this is called a mesocyclone. It can be 10 kilometres wide and spin at 55 km per hr.

03:00 PM

New storms

The clouds did not drop down to the ground so we knew there was not going to be a tornado here. We heard over our radio that there were more storms 240 kilometres away. Perhaps there would be a tornado there.

We turned the cars around.

We drove quickly. We knew that the storms were building up fast and we did not want to miss the tornadoes. We wanted to get in front of them so we could place the turtles.

FACT BOX

In the centre of the United States of America, about one storm in a hundred makes a tornado, during the tornado season.

I saw the swirling clouds. They were very close to the ground and it was very windy. The storm looked dangerous.

FACT BOX

As more warm air feeds into a mesocyclone, it spins round faster and faster. The faster it spins, the tighter it gets. Then a tornado might drop down out of it.

The tornado

Then I saw the tornado. Across the fields, a bright **funnel** of air came spinning down to the ground. It began sucking up the dust – and anything else that got in its way.

The tornado was spinning away from us. All the cars spread out to chase it.

We lost the tornado. We could not see it at all. We were driving through rain now. It was very dark.

06:55 PM

Most tornadoes are only 100 to 200 metres wide. They can move along at a speed of 60 km per hr. But the winds inside them can be spinning at 500 km per hr!

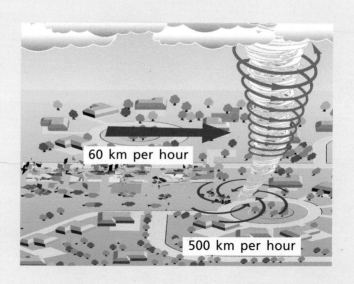

60 km per hour

500 km per hour

When we drove out of the rain,
I looked around. I could not believe
what I saw. Another tornado had
dropped down behind us!

It was a giant! It was heading away
from us across the field. We turned down
a road and raced to get in front of it.

Turtles 1 and 2 in place

We placed the first turtle in the road.
We stopped again, to place the second.

Now the tornado was coming towards us.
It was getting bigger and bigger as it came
closer. It was one of the biggest tornadoes I
had ever seen in my life.

FACT BOX

Tornadoes are often called "**twisters**" because the
winds and clouds in them spin round, so they look as
if they are twisting.

Turtles 3 and 4 in place

We placed the third turtle at a cross-roads. Then we turned up another road to place the fourth. We were just in time. I saw the tornado crossing the road where we had just been.

All four turtles were in place. The tornado seemed to be slowing down. We stopped to look at it. It was massive!

FACT BOX

Many people in the United States of America have tornado shelters in their houses or gardens. These shelters are underground. People stay in them until a tornado has passed.

The farmhouse

The tornado was now very close to a farmhouse. I hoped the people were safe in their tornado shelter. We had put out a tornado warning on TV and on the radio.

FACT BOX

Inside a tornado, the air is spinning upwards. This is why tornadoes suck things up from the ground.

The small tornadoes

The tornado stopped. Three or four small tornadoes had sprung out of it. They were spinning around the outside of the big one. The rain was spinning around and there was lightning. I had never seen anything like this before!

Back at the NSSL.

The big tornado missed our four turtles, but it went over one placed by the other team. That turtle measured it. It was one of the strongest tornadoes ever recorded.

It had been a long day. I looked forward to a hot supper and a good rest.

FACT BOX

Robert Davies-Jones has so far chased about a hundred tornadoes. These storms often bring lightning and huge hailstones with them. It is very dangerous work.

Glossary

funnel A tube, like a cone, which is wide at one end and narrow at the other.

satellite An object which is launched into space by a rocket. It goes round the earth and often carries a camera to gather and send back information.

scientist Someone who does experiments and gathers information to try to find out how our world works.

temperature A measure of how hot or cold it is.

twister Another name for a tornado.

Index